FUNNY JOKES FOR 11 YEAR OLD KIDS

100+ Crazy Jokes That Will Make You Laugh Out Loud!

Cooper the Pooper

TABLE OF CONTENTS

INTRODUCTION

I do not know about you, but I just love telling a good joke and seeing people's faces break into a huge smile. Seeing them start laughing uncontrollably. Seeing them gasping for air because they are laughing so hard.

Seriously, there is nothing better.

To be honest, this was the whole reason that I decided to write this book in the first place.

Ever since I was a little puppy, I loved telling jokes. I would spend all my time searching for new jokes I could share with my friends and family. Hilarious jokes that would have them laughing out loud as soon as they heard the punchline.

But I very quickly noticed that for every good joke I found, I had to read at least ten bad ones (probably more).

And let's face it — there is nothing worse than hearing a bad joke — which is where this book enters the discussion.

I spent years scouring the globe for the funniest jokes on the planet so I could put them in a fantastic book of jokes. A book of jokes that has no bad jokes.

And in your hand, you have the final product. A book that contains the best jokes in the world, designed especially for 11-year-old kids. And no, I am not making up — these jokes are absolutely hilarious.

But wait, there's more.

Something I realized is that the jokes in this book get better the more times you share them. Which means that you should write down your favorites so you can tell them to your friends and family time and time again.

So, what are you waiting for? Start reading the funniest jokes for 11-year-old kids!

CHAPTER 1
FUNNY JOKES

Why don't koalas count as bears?

• **They don't have the right koalafications.**

2

Why aren't dogs good dancers?

• **They have two left feet.**

3

Do you know that some people are scared of Santa?

• **They are Claustrophobic.**

What was the snowman told when he was busted stealing?

• **Freeze!**

5

How do you write a book about Halloween?

- **With a ghostwriter.**

6

What do you call the wife of a hippie?

- **A Mississippi.**

Which is faster: cold or heat?

- **Heat is; you can catch a cold.**

What kind of button won't unbutton?

- **A belly button.**

9

Did you hear about the actor who fell through the floor?

- **It was just a stage he was going through.**

10

Where does Superman love to shop?

- **At the supermarket!**

Why did the banana go to the doctor?

- **It wasn't peeling well.**

Why did the doctor take a red pen to work?

- **In case he wanted to draw blood.**

What shoes does a thief wear?

• **Sneakers.**

What do you call a huge ant?

• **Gi-ant.**

What did the tree say to the wind?

• **Leaf me alone!**

What do skeletons say before a meal?

• **Bone appetite.**

17

What is the color of the wind?

• **Blew.**

18

Why is England the wettest country?

• **Because the queen has reigned there for years.**

19

What did the blanket say to the bed?

- **"Don't worry; I've got you covered."**

20

What do you call a boat that has a hole on the bottom?

- **A sink.**

Why do candles always go on the top of cakes?

• Because it's hard to light them from the bottom.

Why are robots never afraid?

• Because they have nerves of steel.

CHAPTER 2
CRAZY JOKES

Why did the puppy sit in the sun?

- **He wanted to be a hot dog!**

2

Why are baby cows so cute?

- **They are adora-bull!**

Why can't dinosaurs clap?

• **Because they're extinct.**

What do you call a sheep with no legs?

• **A cloud.**

5

Why couldn't the fish play the guitar?

- **You can't tuna-fish.**

6

Why do mice hate swimming?

- **They're scared of catfish.**

What do you call a group of angry elephants?

- **A massive earthquake!**

Why couldn't Dracula sleep?

- **Because of his coffin.**

9

What happens to ice when it gets mad?

• It has a meltdown.

10

What did one flame say to the other?

• We're a perfect match.

What time of year do people get injured the most?

• In the fall.

I was wondering why the ball was getting bigger.

• Then it hit me.

13

What do you call a boy named Lee, who no one talks to?

• **Lonely.**

What did the nose say to the finger?

• **Quit picking on me!**

What is the strongest creature in the world?

• **The snail; it carries its whole house on its back.**

What did the duck say to the waiter?

• **Put it on my bill.**

Why did Johnny throw the clock out of the window?

• **Because he wanted to see time fly.**

When do astronauts eat?

• **At launch time!**

19

How did you find school today?

• **It was there when I got off the bus.**

What do you need to bring to music class?

• **A note-book.**

21

Why did the girl throw a stick of butter out the window?

- **She wanted to see a butterfly.**

Why can't you give Elsa a balloon?

- **She'll let it go.**

CHAPTER 3
LAUGH-OUT-LOUD JOKES

1

Why are camels so good at playing hide and seek?

- **They use camel-flauge!**

2

Why is the bird sad?

- **Because it's a bluebird.**

3

Why did the witch love English as a school subject?

- It taught her how to spell.

4

Why are skeletons evil?

- They are heartless!

5

What did one toilet say to the other?

- **You look a bit flushed!**

6

Did you hear about the two guys who stole a calendar?

- **They each got six months.**

7

Where do ghosts buy their food?

- **At the ghostery store.**

What's the one room a ghost doesn't need in its house?

- **A living room.**

9

Want to hear some roof jokes?

- **This first one's on the house.**

10

Why did the burglar enter the singing contest?

- **He wanted to steal the show.**

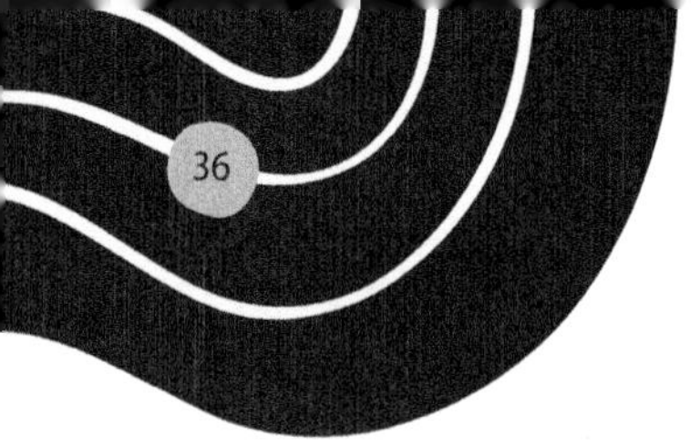

11

What is the best part of a boxer's joke?

- **The punch line.**

12

What is a shark's favorite candy?

- **Jaw breakers.**

13

What do you get when you cross a teacher and a vampire?

• **Lots of blood tests.**

14

Why did the kid study in the airplane?

• **Because he wanted a higher education.**

Why did the chicken cross the playground?

- **To get to the other side.**

What do you call an ant that won't go away?

- **Perman-ant.**

17

Why did the giraffe get bad grades?

- **He always had his head in the clouds.**

18

When do you go on red and stop on green?

- **When you are eating a watermelon.**

19

Why did the chemistry teacher stop telling jokes?

- **She never got a reaction.**

20

Why did the broom get a poor grade in school?

- **Because it was always sweeping during class.**

Do the buses here run on time?

- **No, they run on wheels.**

Why did the leaf go to the doctor?

- **It was feeling green.**

CHAPTER 4
KNOCK-KNOCK JOKES

Knock, knock!

Who's there?

Dorris.

Dorris who?

The Dorris open;close it.

Knock, knock!

Who's there?

Harry.

Harry who?

Harry up — I need to pee!

3

Knock, knock!

Who's there?

Carrie.

Carrie who?

Can you Carrie these bags with me, please!

4

Knock, knock!

Who's there?

Alex.

Alex who?

Alex-plain when you give me a chance!

5

Knock, knock!

Who's there?

Donna.

Donna who?

Donna where I put my keys. Can you help me find them?

6

Knock, knock!

Who's there?

Justin.

Justin who?

Justin time for a party.

7

Knock, knock!

Who's there?

Candice.

Candice who?

Candice door open already?!

8

Knock, knock!

Who's there?

Ben.

Ben who?

Ben hoping you would finally open this door!

9

Knock, knock!

Who's there?

Morris.

Morris who?

The Morris the merrier.

10

Knock, knock!

Who's there?

Leaf.

Leaf who?

Don't leaf me out here knocking all day!

Knock, knock!

Who's there?

Anita.

Anita who?

Anita come inside; it's pouring out here!

12

Knock, knock!

Who's there?

Owls.

Owls who?

Sure they do!

13

Knock, knock!

Who's there?

Turnip.

Turnip who?

Turnip the sound; I love this song!

14

Knock, knock!

Who's there?

Broccoli.

Broccoli who?

You expect a broccoli to have a last name?!

15

Knock, knock!

Who's there?

Yukon.

Yukon who?

Yukon say that again!

16

Knock, knock!

Who's there?

Sam.

Sam who?

Sam person whose been knocking for 10 minutes now.

17

Knock, knock!

Who's there?

Hada.

Hada who?

Hada great time!

18

Knock, knock!

Who's there?

Max.

Max who?

Max no difference — just open the door!

Knock, knock!

Who's there?

Sweden.

Sweden who?

Sweden the coffee; it's too bitter!

Knock, knock!

Who's there?

Dozen.

Dozen who?

Dozen anyone want to let me in?

Knock, knock!

Who's there?

Ireland.

Ireland who?

Ireland you my umbrella; you'll need it.

22

Knock, knock!

Who's there?

Voodoo.

Voodoo who?

Voodoo you think you are, asking me so many questions?

CHAPTER 5
BONUS
JOKES

1

What's the hardest thing about learning to ride a horse?

- **The ground.**

2

Why didn't the orange win the race?

- **It ran out of juice!**

How many cherries grow on a cherry tree?

- **All of them.**

What do you call a dentist who fixes crocodile's teeth?

- **Totally crazy.**

What do you call a bee that isn't sure?

• **A may-bee.**

Why do zebras like to watch old movies?

• **Because they're black and white.**

When does a doctor get mad?

- **When he runs out of patients!**

What do ghosts like to eat in the summer?

- **I scream.**

On what day are ghosts most scary?

- **Fright-day!**

10

What do ghosts do at sleepovers?

- **They tell scary human stories!**

11

What does Dracula like to watch on TV?

• **Neck-flix!**

12

Which fruit is a vampire's favorite?

• **A neck-tarine.**

Where do ghosts live?

- **They don’t.**

Why didn't the lamp sink?

- **It was too light.**

Why do bicycles fall over?

- **Because they're two-tired.**

16

What did one knife say to the other knife?

- **You're looking sharp today!**

17

Why was the remote control annoyed?

• **Because everyone was pushing its buttons.**

18

What goes up, but doesn't come back down?

• **Your age.**

19

Why couldn't the sailor learn his alphabet?

- **Because he always got lost at C.**

20

Why did the cow wear a bell?

- **Her horn wasn't working.**

FINAL WORDS

Thank you for taking the time to read my book.

I spent years travelling the world looking the best jokes for 11-year-old kids I could find — so nothing makes me happier than knowing that great kids like you are reading them.

But remember, there is more work to do.

At the start of this book, I said these jokes get funnier the more times you share them — and now it is time to share them.

So, take a deep breath and head back to the start of this book. Turn the pages and pick your favorite jokes so you can share them with your friends and family — after all, the only thing better than hearing a funny joke is telling a funny joke.

What are you waiting for — head back to the start and get ready to laugh again and again.

Printed in Great Britain
by Amazon